LIFE AND TIMES IN
ANCIENT GREECE

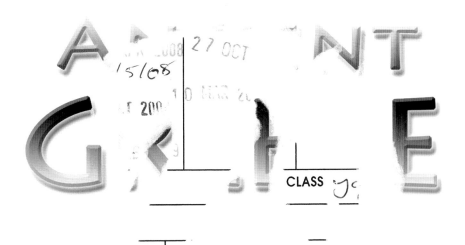

KINGFISHER

Kingfisher Publications Plc
New Penderel House
283–288 High Holborn
London WC1V 7HZ
www.kingfisherpub.com

Based on material first published in the Sightseers series
by Kingfisher Publications Plc 1999

This edition first published by Kingfisher Publications Plc 2007
2 4 6 8 10 9 7 5 3 1

1TR/0607/TIMS/(MA)/140MA/C

Written and edited by: Julie Ferris, Conrad Mason
Consultant: David Nightingale
Production controller: Aysun Ackay
DTP manager: Nicky Studdart

Illustrations by: Inklink Firenze and Kevin Maddison

A CIP catalogue record for this book
is available from the British Library.

ISBN 978 0 7534 1557 3 (paperback)
ISBN 978 0 7534 1626 6 (hardback)

Printed in China

Contents

Greek civilization

The ancient Greek civilization was made up of small, independent city-states on the coasts of the Mediterranean. From around 500BCE the Greeks began to experience a golden age. Peace between warring cities allowed arts, theatre, science and philosophy to flourish. Greek achievements in these fields have had a lasting impact on the world.

◁ The great statesman Pericles (c. 495–429BCE) was a general of the Athenian army. He helped to bring about the Golden Age through his victories against the Persians and his brilliant diplomacy. This book is about Greece in 432BCE, in the time of Pericles.

From around 1600–1100BCE, the Mycenaeans were very powerful in Greece. They made beautiful gold treasures.

The Greek Dark Ages lasted from 1100–800BCE. During this time Greeks began settling around the Mediterranean.

The Olympic Games were first recorded in 776BCE, although they probably began a long time before this date.

▽ Dominating the skyline of Athens is the Acropolis. Once a hilltop fort, it later became the site of the Parthenon, a great temple to the goddess Athena, built to celebrate the Greek victory over Persia.

▽ People had been living in the Mediterranean for centuries before the Golden Age. The Romans conquered Greece in 146BCE, ending its power.

The powerful city-state of Athens was ruled by democracy, which meant that all male citizens could take part in the government of the city. Other city-states, such as Sparta, were ruled by kings or small groups of noble aristocrats. In around 480BCE the Greeks came together in a league to defeat the Persians. However, after the war Athens took over the league and turned it into the Athenian empire. It kept control over the other Greeks using its powerful navy, and became the largest and most important of the city-states.

A system of democracy evolved in Athens. All male citizens were given a say in how the state was governed.

From around 500BCE, many Greek city-states were locked in war with Persia, a powerful Middle Eastern empire.

In 448BCE the Greeks won the Persian Wars. This revived Athens' culture and the Acropolis was rebuilt.

Transport

Greece is made up of many islands, and the Greeks were great sailors. The Athenian harbour, Piraeus, was the biggest port in the Mediterranean. Journeys by land were much harder and involved long, steep treks by donkey over the mountainous inland regions.

◁ Greeks who had to travel inland hired a donkey. They wore wide-brimmed straw hats to protect themselves from the hot sun.

△ Big eyes were often painted on the front of Greek ships to scare away evil spirits and protect the sailors.

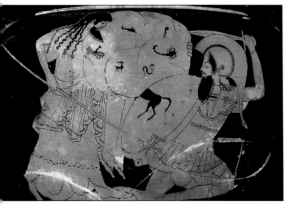

Travel was extremely dangerous in ancient Greece. At sea, pirates waited to plunder slow merchant vessels. On land, bands of robbers attacked and stole from travellers.

◁ Poseidon, god of the sea, carried a trident – a spear with three prongs. Greeks believed he could prevent shipwrecks and so made offerings of wine to him.

During the Greek winter, travel practically came to a halt. Winters tended to be very wet, making mountain tracks impassable. Sailing also became difficult because boat sails got wet and visibility was poor.

△ Travellers inland would often take a break from the rough, stony roads to stay in an inn, where they were safe from robbers. However, this could also be risky – Greek comedy writers often included jokes about cheating innkeepers in their plays!

Clothing

The basic dress for Greek men and women was a chiton (pronounced 'kye-ton'). Made from linen or wool, the chiton was little more than a tube of material pinned or sewn over the shoulders. In the countryside people often wore a simple tunic secured with a belt, and hats in hot weather.

◁ To take a shower, Greeks sat in a large pottery bowl while a slave poured water over them.

▷ Over their chiton Greeks often draped a hard-wearing woollen cloak called a himation. It was a sign of good breeding and elegance to have the himation arranged correctly. These garments were expensive to make and so were a popular target for thieves.

▷ Greek women wore their chitons to the ankle and dyed them bright colours such as red, green or purple.

▷ Women were rarely allowed to leave the house. When they did they wore their finest jewellery. Hairpins, earrings and rings were sold by travelling pedlars.

Greek men usually had beards and kept their hair short, except for the Spartans, who grew their hair long to make themselves more terrifying in battle. Greek women tied their hair up in carefully arranged styles and wore lots of make-up. Sometimes they wore high-heeled sandals to make themselves look taller.

▷ Greeks went barefoot at home, but wore leather sandals in the street. These were made by cobblers. Customers would stand on the leather while the cobbler drew round their feet.

The Greeks thought that pale skin and blonde hair were beautiful. Poor women who had suntans from working outside would often paint their faces with white lead to look paler. Some women also bleached their hair to become fair.

9

Food and drink

Bread, gruel, olives, figs and cheese made from goat's milk were the most common foods in ancient Greece. Cheap fish was available in coastal towns, but meat was too expensive for most people.

▽ Professional cooks were hired for symposions. Slaves were sent out with invitations – small statues showing people eating or walking to a feast.

Wealthy Greeks held elaborate dinner parties called symposions. The guests lay on couches and enjoyed a lavish three-course meal. Popular dishes included piglet stuffed with thrushes, egg yolks with oysters, and quinces cooked in honey and baked in a tart.

▽ Wine was drunk from a broad, shallow cup called a kylix. Drinking games were very popular.

▽ In most families, women prepared all the food. Cooking was done over a charcoal fire using bronze or clay utensils.

At a symposion dinner, slaves were on hand to cut up the guests' food, and sometimes even feed them. After the meal, acrobats, dancing girls and musicians performed, and vast quantities of wine were drunk. Guests told stories and jokes, and often discussed politics. Female visitors were not invited to a symposion. The only women allowed to attend were slaves and entertainers.

▽ Poor people had a more basic diet than the rich, but could eat meat at religious festivals.

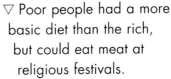

The agora

The agora, or market-place, was the centre of city life. Greek men spent most of the day there, discussing politics, doing business or meeting with friends. Meat, fish, vegetables and fruit were on sale, together with pottery, bronze goods, textiles and even slaves. Above the Athenian agora was a temple to Hephaistos, the god of metalworking.

▷ Local craftsmen sold finely carved marble figures and bronze statues in the agora, as well as pottery bowls, vases and cups. These were often painted with gods, heroes or scenes from daily life.

◁ This Athenian coin has a picture of Athena, goddess of the city, on one side. On the other side is her emblem, an owl.

Around the agora ran the stoa – long, sheltered collonades. Shoemakers, ironmongers, carpenters, money-lenders and doctors could all be found here, as well as the offices of lawyers and magistrates. Religious and political speakers gave speeches from the stoa.

▷ In the stoa people talked about philosophy or told tales of gods and heroes. The most famous stories, the *Iliad* and the *Odyssey*, still exist today. They tell of a war between Greece and Troy.

Homes

While temples and monuments were made of marble, ordinary houses were built with mud bricks and had tiled roofs. Most of the rooms were on one floor and were built around an open-air courtyard where the family ate its meals. Most families had a shrine in the courtyard where they worshipped the gods.

▽ Burglary was common in ancient Egypt. The mud bricks used to build houses were soft enough for thieves to cut through the walls and break in. People kept their valuables hidden for protection.

△ Many households had slaves. Male slaves guarded the house and did the shopping. Female slaves did the cooking and cleaning.

▽ Most Greek furniture was three-legged. It could stand on any surface, even bumpy earth floors.

▽ In the courtyard, women could relax and chat to one another, while children played games.

△ Clay lamps were lit at night. Oil was poured in the middle and a wick was put in the spout.

Women stayed at home for most of the day. They were only allowed to leave for short periods of time, and were not even supposed to open the outer door of the house in case they came face to face with a man. Girls learnt to run the house by helping their mothers.

The theatre

Drama was invented in Athens as part of the spring festival for the god Dionysus. At the time of Pericles, the city's semicircular theatre could hold over 10,000 people, and performances were held once a month. These events began at dawn and lasted for the whole day, with several plays being performed. There were serious dramas called tragedies, and boisterous, often vulgar plays known as comedies.

△ Some seats had game boards to keep spectators amused in between plays.

▷ Spectators stamped and whistled to show appreciation. Theatre staff hit people with sticks if they were being too noisy.

△ Actors used masks to show which character they were playing. Masks were usually made of linen or leather, and sometimes had human hair attached.

In a tragedy, three actors played all the various speaking roles, changing their masks whenever they became a different character. A chorus of up to 15 performers sang or chanted a commentary on the action. They were led by the choregos, a wealthy citizen who paid for their training and their costumes. Although women were allowed to go to the theatre, only men were allowed to act. They played both male and female roles.

◁ Plays often included music. The lyre, which is similar to a harp, was the most popular instrument.

The assembly

Democracy means rule by the people, and in Athens every citizen had a say in the running of the city. They debated important matters at the assembly, held on the slopes of the Pynx Hill about every nine days. Decisions counted if there were at least 6,000 citizens present.

△ To prevent anyone speaking for too long during a debate, speeches were timed with a water clock.

△ Greeks took the assembly very seriously. Citizens were herded in with rope dipped in red dye. Anyone who was too slow got paint on their clothes and had to pay a fine.

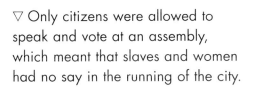

Although any man was allowed to stand up and make a speech, it was usually only the confident and well-educated that dared to do it. Rival speakers jeered at each other and tried to persuade the crowd that their ideas were the best. Slave archers kept order and prevented fights from breaking out. When a matter had been fully debated, citizens voted by raising their hands.

▷ In an Athenian trial, juries voted by dropping bronze ballots with hollow (guilty) or solid (innocent) shafts into a box. By holding the ballot between finger and thumb, people could hide which way they were voting.

Trials in Athens were often rowdy, as jurors were allowed to shout questions at the defendants or prosecutors. The juries were very large – sometimes thousands in the most important cases. This made them difficult to bribe. After all the evidence had been heard, the jurors voted for whoever they thought had presented the most convincing argument.

The Acropolis

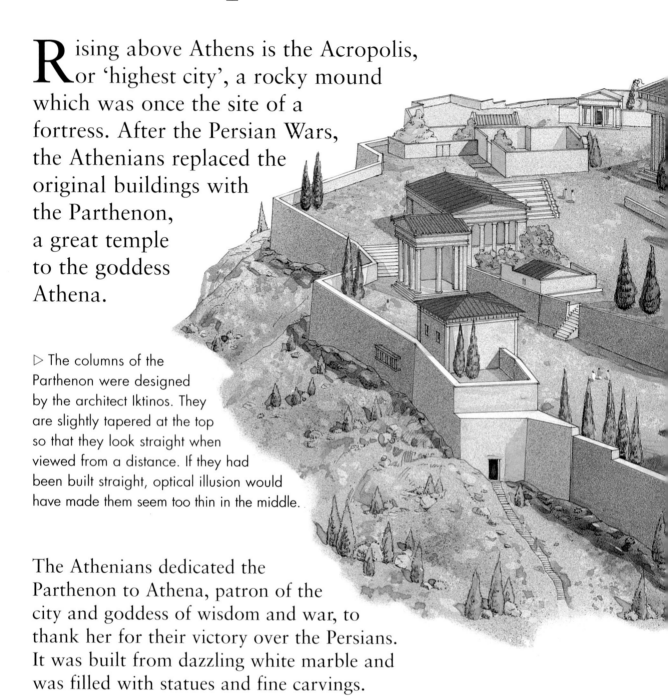

Rising above Athens is the Acropolis, or 'highest city', a rocky mound which was once the site of a fortress. After the Persian Wars, the Athenians replaced the original buildings with the Parthenon, a great temple to the goddess Athena.

▷ The columns of the Parthenon were designed by the architect Iktinos. They are slightly tapered at the top so that they look straight when viewed from a distance. If they had been built straight, optical illusion would have made them seem too thin in the middle.

The Athenians dedicated the Parthenon to Athena, patron of the city and goddess of wisdom and war, to thank her for their victory over the Persians. It was built from dazzling white marble and was filled with statues and fine carvings.

◁ Greeks took great care in decorating large temples such as the Acropolis. This temple carving shows images of the gods. The seated figure is Zeus, king of all the gods.

▽ The Parthenon was decorated with friezes commemorating the Panathenaia festival, held every July in honour of Athena. There was singing, dancing, athletics and a temple procession.

Inside the temple was a vast statue of Athena, made out of gold and ivory. Athena became patron of the city after winning a contest with Poseidon. She was said to have given Athens the gift of the olive tree, a symbol of prosperity.

▷ Visitors to the Parthenon could drink from special coin-operated water dispensers.

The Olympic Games

△ The gods were believed to live in the clouds above Mount Olympus. Although named after the mountain, Olympia was a long way from it.

The Olympic Games were held every four years at Olympia in honour of Zeus, king of the gods. Athletes travelled from all over the Mediterranean to compete. Events included running, chariot racing, long jump, javelin, discus and fighting.

▽ The fiercest event at the Games was the pankration, a cross between boxing and wrestling. The rules allowed anything except eye-gouging and biting.

▽ The pentathlon was a special event that included five different sports. It was supposed to determine who was the best overall athlete.

◁ Because the athletes competed naked, women were not allowed to watch the Games under any circumstances. Separate, women-only games were held in honour of the goddess Hera, wife of Zeus.

The stadium at Olympia had room for about 40,000 spectators. The judges had seats, and the other spectators stood or sat on the surrounding hillside. Dancers and jugglers entertained the crowds in between events, and there were food stalls for refreshments. Wearing a hat was forbidden in case it blocked someone's view.

◁ Victorious athletes won a wreath of olive leaves cut from a sacred tree.

23

Sparta

While the Athenians had the most powerful navy in Greece, the city-state of Sparta had the toughest soldiers. Its entire culture was based on maintaining a full-time army. Spartans did not work and had no holidays. Their lives were an endless cycle of tough military drills and exercises.

△ The Spartans valued bravery more than anything. If a man was thought to be cowardly, he had half his hair and beard shaved off and was jeered at in the street.

All Spartan citizens had to do 23 years' compulsory military training. Land slaves called helots worked the fields to produce food. Helots were despised and treated cruelly.

24

Family life was not important to the Spartans. They believed that warriors should be loyal to their community and not to their relations. Boys were sent to military school at the age of seven, and lived and trained there until the end of their military service. They were forced to endure as much hardship as possible to toughen them up. Sometimes they even had contests to see who could withstand being whipped for the longest.

▽ Women in Sparta were expected to exercise and keep fit so that they would produce strong, healthy babies.

Spartans learnt to move stealthily in the dark, to steal food and to live with few clothes or possessions. They were discouraged from reading books so that they would not think too much.

◁ Spartan soldiers were very organized and disciplined. In battle they used a formation called a phalanx, attacking side by side in tight rows, and using their shields to protect the man on their left.

25

The countryside

△ Fishermen used trawling nets out at sea, and fishing rods in lakes and rivers.

Most Athenians owned small farms in the country. The soil was not very fertile, but people made the most of the land by growing fig trees, vines, olive trees, wheat and barley. The countryside was also full of small villages and temples.

▽ Farmers beat olive branches with a stick to make the ripe fruit fall to the floor. Then the olives were put in a press and oil was squeezed from them.

Greek cities would sometimes send
messengers to a distant temple to ask
advice from an oracle – a priest
who spoke to the gods. The
gods gave the priest clues
about what would happen
in the future. The most
famous oracle in Greece
was the priestess at the
Temple of Apollo in
Delphi. Greeks consulted her
when they were making important
decisions, or planning to go to war.

▷ The oracle
at Delphi spoke
to Apollo
when she was
in a trance. The
god communicated
with her in riddles
which were then
translated by priests.

Greek society

There were many important roles in Greek society, from doctors and teachers to lawyers and policemen. Hard labour was carried out by slaves, who were usually foreigners. Despite rivalry between individual city-states, all Greeks thought of themselves as superior to foreigners.

Good health was considered the greatest gift that the gods gave to man, and medicine was very sophisticated. Doctors examined the patient's symptoms, their diet and whether they exercised, before prescribing herbal cures. Greeks admired Egyptian medicine, but were more scientific than the Egyptians.

△ Laws were often inscribed on stone tablets or walls. Most boys learned how to read and write using pieces of bark and ink made from soot.

△ One doctor, Hippocrates of Cos, taught medicine and even wrote down the proper methods that doctors should follow.

In most city-states the ruling king kept control with his soldiers. The Spartans had two kings at a time, and used bands of warriors to scare their slaves so that they would not rebel. In Athens the police force was made up of foreign slaves from Scythia. They could be recognised by their soft cloth caps and bows and arrows.

The Athenians had a special system to get rid of any citizen who had become so powerful that he was a threat to the democracy. This was called ostracism – banishment from Athens for a period of ten years. If the ostracized citizen returned before the ten years were up, he was put to death.

△ Citizens voted using small pieces of broken pottery called ostraka, on which they scratched the name of the person that they wanted to ostracize.

Every year a meeting was held and citizens were invited to write down the name of the person they most wanted to leave the city. If at least 6,000 people wrote the same man's name, he was ostracized.

◁ The ostraka were collected in large urns before being counted.

Quiz

Now that you've seen what life was like in ancient Greece, test your knowledge with this quiz. Remember, you can always turn back if you want to look for the information. Answers can be found on page 32.

1. Why did Greeks usually travel by boat rather than going overland?

a) Because it was very expensive to hire a donkey to carry the luggage.

b) Because the inland regions were very mountainous and difficult to cross.

c) Because Greeks did not want to upset Poseidon, the god of the sea.

2. Why were women with pale skin thought to be beautiful in ancient Greece?

a) It showed that they came from such a wealthy family that they did not need to work outside in the sun.

b) The Greeks were worried about the harmful effects of sun on the skin.

c) Pale skin complemented their brightly coloured chitons.

3. Why did Greek furniture often have only three legs?

a) Three-legged furniture could stand more firm on bumpy earth floors.

b) Wood was so scarce in Greece that it was too expensive to make furniture with four legs.

c) The number three had religious importance.

4. How did Greeks show their appreciation at the theatre?

a) By clapping their hands.

b) By shouting at the actors.

c) By whistling and stamping their feet.

5. Who spoke at an assembly?

a) Any Greek.

b) Any citizen of the city-state of Athens.

c) Aristocrats and important citizens.

6. Spartan men had to do 23 years' military training. Why were Spartan women expected to exercise and keep fit?

a) So that they would produce strong and healthy babies.

b) So that they would be ready to fight and defend Sparta against attack.

c) So that they would be strong enough to stop the helots (the slaves that worked the fields and cooked the food) from rebelling.

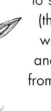

7. An assembly was called in Athens roughly once every nine days. Who had the job of keeping order at the assembly?

a) Officials elected by the assembly each year.

b) The oldest citizens at the assembly.

c) Slave archers.

8. Greeks believed there was a family of gods. Where did they believe that the gods lived?

a) In the clouds above Mount Olympus.

b) In the Parthenon temple on the Acropolis.

c) In the sea.

9. The Olympic Games were held in Olympia every four years. What prize was presented to the triumphant winners at the Games?

a) A large sum of money.

b) A wreath of olive leaves cut from a sacred tree.

c) A medal made of gold.

10. To find out what the future had in store, Greeks sometimes travelled to Delphi and consulted the oracle.
What was the oracle?

a) An ancient prophecy inscribed on tablets of stone.

b) A statue of the god Apollo.

c) A priestess who had the power to speak to the gods.

Index

Acknowledgements

Design assistance
Joanne Brown

Inklink Firenze illustrators
Simone Boni, Alessandro Rabatti, Lorenzo Pieri, Luigi Critone, Lucia Mattioli, Francisco Petracchi, Theo Caneschi.

Additional illustrations
Vanessa Card, Terry Gabbey, Ian Jackson, Nicki Palin, David Salariya/Shirley Willis, Thomas Trojer.

Picture credits
b = bottom, c = centre, l = left, r = right, t = top
4c British Museum/Michael Holford; 6bl Vienna Kunsthistorisches Museum/AKG London; 9tr British Museum/Michael Holford; 11tr Ancient Art and Architecture, tl Corbis UK/Araldo de Luca; 13c AKG London; 15cr British Museum; 16tr Ancient Art & Architecture; 19cr American School of Classical Studies, Athens; 21tr British Museum/Michael Holford; 22tl Corbis UK/Robert Gill; 23tl British Museum/Michael Holford; 25tr British Museum/Michael Holford; 26tl Erich Lessing/AKG London; 28cr British Museum/Michael Holford; 29tr Corbis UK/Gianni Dagli Orti.

The publisher would like to thank the following for permission to reproduce their material. Every care has been taken to trace copyright holders. However, if there have been unintentional omissions or failure to trace copyright holders, we apologize and will, if informed, endeavour to make corrections in any future edition.

Quiz answers

1 b) 2 a) 3 a) 4 c) 5 b) 6 a) 7 c) 8 a) 9 b) 10 c)